Baffling &
Bizarre
INVENTIONS

JIM MURPHY

SKY PONY PRESS • NEW YORK

Contents

Introduction

The earliest settlements in America were surrounded by a vast, seemingly impenetrable forest that covered the east coast from Florida to Canada and went inland for hundreds and hundreds of miles. Few people lived here then, roads were wretched when they existed, and communications were virtually nonexistent. When William Bradford described the New World in his 1630 history *Of Plymoth Plantation,* he called it a "hideous and desolate wilderness full of wild beasts and wild men."

How did men and women cope with these strange, harsh surroundings? Many didn't. Some died, the result of disease, an occasional hostile Indian, or simple stupidity. Others waited for the next ship and fled back to their homelands in civilized Europe. Most, however, chose to stay and face obstacles with stubborn determination. They confronted their problems head on for a very good reason: either they solved them or they went hungry.

Logical ingenuity often helped ensure survival, and the development of the Kentucky long rifle is a perfect example of this. Before the Kentucky long rifle, the gun the colonists used was the primitive matchlock, a weapon requiring over fifteen steps to set off and so heavy it had to be mounted on a stand. When the rifle fired (something not at all guaranteed in rain or snow), it made a great noise and flash. Unfortunately, it was so inaccurate that hitting any target, especially one that moved, was more a matter of incredible luck than skill.

But Americans needed a more reliable weapon in order to survive, a fact that might seem strange to many people today. Just remember that there were no supermarkets or shopping malls back then, and no standing army or police either. Settlers living apart from a village had to have a way to defend themselves; game was often their only source of meat, while animal furs and skins had to be used for shoes and clothing.

As the population increased to 300,000 by 1710, so did the demand, and the market, for better rifles. It was this possibility of profit that prompted German settlers in western Pennsylvania to fashion a different sort of rifle around 1720.

They improved the firing mechanism so the rifle would always go off. They also lengthened the barrel to four feet and cut spiral grooves inside it called "rifling" (European gunsmiths knew about rifling in the sixteenth century but had never applied the concept with much determination). Rifling made the bullet spin, which allowed for more precise aim. One problem with rifling was that the bullet had to fit very snugly for it to catch in the groove and spin. The German craftsmen's solution was straightforward and brilliant: they wrapped the lead shot in a patch of greased leather. The resulting tight fit worked. What's more, a backwoodsman could make his own shot without too much concern for exact tooling. The final product was a nine-pound rifle, easy to carry and fire, and accurate up to 300 yards!

The Kentucky long rifle was an early attempt to confront and control the "wilderness" through invention. Other attempts followed. In fact, Americans have produced more than 4 ½ million patented inventions over the past 200 years, one of the greatest outpourings of practical creativity in history. The list is endless, but includes such well-known items as the safety pin, telephone, elevator, screw-top jar, baseball glove, airplane, barbed wire, and record player.

What follows is a quiz involving forty-five of the lesser-known, though much funnier, inventions (including several from Europe, proof that inventiveness and humor existed elsewhere). Patent drawings and magazine illustrations give the visual clue. A written clue, plus a number of possible answers, are provided to aid you in your guessing. Study the clues carefully; try to imagine how the gadget might have worked and what the inventor was thinking when he assembled it. Then turn the page to see if your answer is correct.

Don't be afraid to laugh during the quiz. After all, these inventions aren't called "baffling and bizarre" for no reason! On the other hand, try not to judge these machines too severely, no matter how outrageous they may appear. Each represents an individual's attempt to make life a little easier or safer or more fun. A visitor to the United States, Alexis de Tocqueville, noted this unstoppable drive. "It would seem," he wrote in his book *Democracy in America, 1835-1840,* "as if in the United States every man's power of invention was on the stretch to find new ways of increasing the wealth and satisfying the needs of the public. ..." And maybe more than anything else it's this spirit of inventiveness, coupled with our willingness to laugh at ourselves, that truly unites us even today.

chapter one

The Animal Kingdom

It was lightweight and could be strapped onto an animal quickly. What's more, this 1857 invention helped the animal through some tough times.

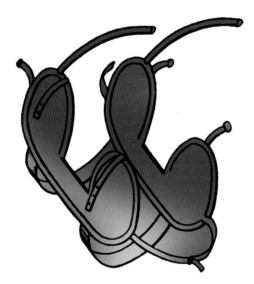

1. A life preserver for horses
2. A portable feeding machine for horses, cows, and other farm creatures
3. A heating device for pets

A LIFE PRESERVER FOR HORSES

Nineteenth-century horse soldiers frequently chased bandits and rustlers across rough terrain. Often they would come to a wide, deep river. Since the army carried heavy equipment, they had to use boats to cross the water, which allowed the lighter-traveling bandits to escape. To eliminate long delays, William Ernest created two large rubber bags, each with a rubber hose. The hose allowed the soldier to inflate the bag with air. They were then strapped to the horse's stomach.

"A squadron of cavalry thus equipped . . . can cross rivers, lakes or estuaries in safety, without the aid of boats." Ernest suggested that each soldier bring along a pair of waterproof pants and boots to ensure a pleasantly dry crossing for himself.

This 1963 device was strapped on a cow's face. With it in position, you had a truly contented animal.

1. A pair of eyeglasses
2. An antifly guard
3. A mechanism to help cows sleep during the day

David Hersh loved dogs, so he invented this article of clothing for them in 1965. As long as Fido wore it, the owner had one less worry.

1. Running shorts for greyhounds
2. A flotation device for large dogs
3. A rear-end warmer for chihuahuas
4. Training pants for dogs

AN ANTIFLY GUARD

Henry George O'Hare wanted to solve an age-old problem. Whenever flies buzzed around a cow's face, the cow became skittish. It swished its tail, shook its head, and danced around in an effort to chase away the insects. This was not a problem if the cow was by itself in an open field. But it could be upsetting and dangerous to the person trying to milk the cow.

O'Hare's solution was a leather mask with a see-through wire-mesh screen. The mask prevented insects from flying near the cow's face, which kept the animal calm. A placid cow was easier to milk, O'Hare pointed out, and gave sweeter milk.

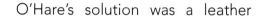

TRAINING PANTS FOR DOGS

A dog can be an adorable pet, but if it hasn't been housebroken, a mess is guaranteed. Hersh stated that the pants were to be secured to "the posterior of the dog's abdomen for a period of time during which the dog was restrained from depositing metabolic waste" on the rug.

Joseph Barad and Edward E. Markoff saw a real need for their 1908 invention. It consisted of wire, springs, a trap door, a bell, and feeding station. An animal entered one side and sent the device—and the animal—into action.

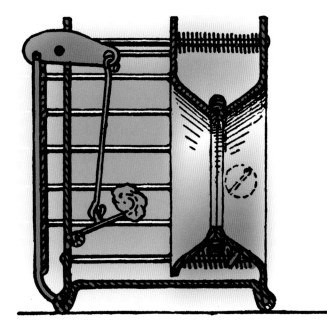

1. An automatic feeder for dogs and cats
2. A hamster exercise machine
3. A device that allows dogs to open doors
4. A rattrap

A RATTRAP

Getting rid of rats or mice in a house is troublesome. Poisons might be eaten by pets or small children and the use of a spring-action trap is often messy. This invention did away with unwanted rodents in a clean way.

The rodent is lured to the trap by bait on a hook. In order to eat the food, the rodent must stick its neck through a round hole. When the rat touches the food, a spring snaps a collar around its neck. Attached to the collar is a bell. According to inventors Barad and Markoff, the ringing of the bell would startle the animal and send it sprinting back to its nest, "thereby frightening the other rats and causing them to flee as well."

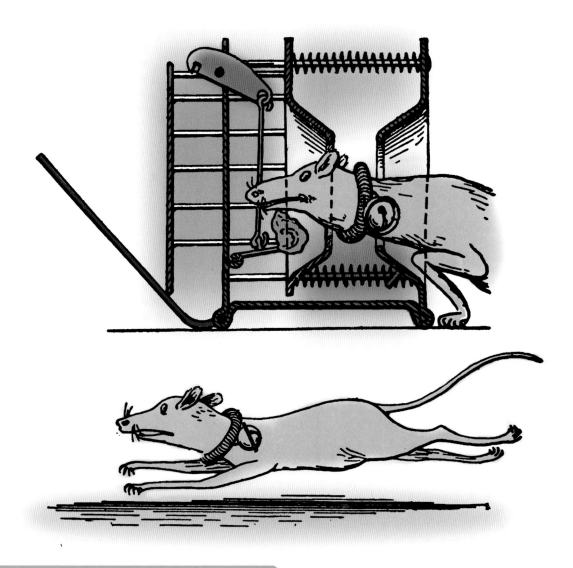

A bull is a large, ungainly, and sometimes headstrong animal. But fasten on this metal device and his character will change.

1. A piece of jewelry for bulls
2. An antibutting device
3. A device for herding bulls by radio waves
4. A radio for transmitting soothing music

This invention could be made of lightweight cloth or plastic and was to be strapped on a chicken. It had a function you could count on.

1. A chest protector for fighting cocks
2. A carrying handle for chickens and large birds
3. An egg counter
4. An automatic feather plucker

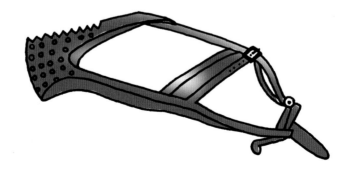

AN ANTIBUTTING DEVICE

Bulls butt doors, gates, fences, barn walls, and each other. Lenard Pemberton hoped his 1967 invention would put a stop to this destructive habit.

Made of very strong chain links with a metal crossbar, this device was fastened to the bull's horns and nose ring. Two sharp, circular spurs were attached to each side of the bar. When the bull butted anything, the spurs dug into his forehead. Pemberton claimed the spurs were not sharp enough to cut the animal, but they would hurt enough to prevent the bull from butting again.

AN EGG COUNTER

It is very important for a farmer to know exactly how many eggs each hen lays. If a hen becomes unproductive, it isn't economical to keep it. Counting eggs is a simple task if there are twenty or thirty hens. But when the coop has hundreds or thousands of them, it is impossible for a farmer to count the eggs himself.

Hans Eugen Birch-Iensen believed his 1964 invention was the solution. The counter was strapped on the hen. A circular hoop was located beneath the bird's tail. The hoop had a small plastic counting device attached to it. As an egg passed through the hoop it hit a tiny prong that clicked the counter ahead one number. A farmer could check the hen's counter every week or so. A hen that produced a lot of eggs remained in the coop. Those that didn't ended up on the dinner table.

chapter two

What You Wear

The coat has changed very little in the last one hundred years. You put one arm in each sleeve, then button the front to keep out the cold or rain. But in 1953 Howard C. Ross had a big idea.

1. An overcoat for two people
2. A combination raincoat and tent
3. A coat for a very fat person

AN OVERCOAT FOR TWO PEOPLE

Ross and a friend were walking down the street when it started to rain. Ross was wearing a coat, but his friend wasn't. As the rain came down and his friend got wetter and wetter, Ross had an idea for such emergencies.

Ross's coat looks very ordinary most of the time. But when it rains or snows, the wearer can undo a series of clasps, expand the coat, and invite a friend inside. Ross felt his coat would be particularly handy at outdoor sporting events.

Hats were very popular at the beginning of the twentieth century, but wearing a hat could cause problems. Frank L. Snow of Los Angeles thought he had solved one with his 1914 invention.

1. An antitheft mechanism
2. A miniature radio
3. A clasp to secure hat to head on windy days

This 1912 invention allowed a person to go through an entire day without concern.

1. A portable lightning rod
2. A hat support
3. An AM-FM radio receiver
4. A wearable billboard

AN ANTITHEFT MECHANISM

When hats were in fashion, a man would enter a restaurant and put his hat on a rack, confident it would be there when he had finished his meal. But all too often, the man would discover that his hat had been stolen. This happened three times to Snow, so he invented an antitheft mechanism.

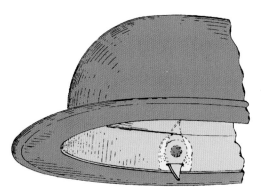

The device consisted of a one-inch-wide metal cap with a very sharp barb inside. A person clicked the barb into the down position before hanging up the hat. The barb could not be retracted unless the combination to the tiny lock on the side of the cap was known. A thief might still steal the hat, Snow said in his patent application, but if he tried to put it on he'd get a very painful jab for his crime.

A HAT SUPPORT

As with the bustle, any fashion trend can become distorted. If it was considered elegant to wear a flowered or feathered hat, then it must, some reasoned, be even more elegant to wear a *very large* flowered hat, but large hats were heavy and hard to keep on, especially when a gust of wind sprang up. Louisiana's Arthur Munchauren's invention consisted of sturdy metal braces that ensured the hat would stay firmly in place even on breezy days. In addition, Munchauren felt the

supports "allow free circulation of air around and over head, thus to prevent headaches caused by weight of hats." What if it rained? The inventor advised women to put a rubber bag over their hat and head!

This 1877 invention was supposed to be worn around the neck. Using it was as simple as breathing.

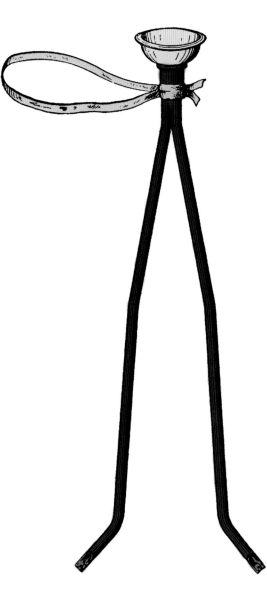

1. A device for catching and disposing of drool
2. An amplifier for the hard of hearing
3. An automatic foot warmer
4. A feeding tube for twins

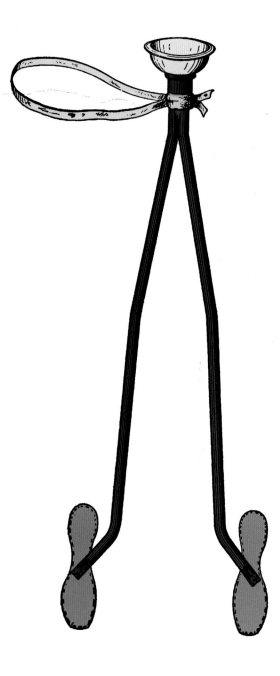

AN AUTOMATIC FOOT WARMER

W. T. Steiger was tired of walking around with cold feet. "It is well-established," wrote Steiger in his patent, "that our lungs constitute the laboratory of nature, within which animal heat is generated and distributed to other parts of the body by the action of the heart and circulation of the blood." But our feet, the inventor went on to note with some alarm, are short-changed of heat because of their distance from the lungs.

To offset this injustice, Steiger fashioned a long rubber tube to be inserted in the side of each shoe. As the user strolled along he would breathe into the funnel and the warm air would be channeled directly to the feet.

The top of this 1877 invention opened wide for easy access. Once the top was closed, what was inside remained safe for quite a while.

1. A life jacket
2. A robot oven for delivery of hot pizzas
3. An antipollution suit for city dwellers
4. A space suit

A LIFE JACKET

The nineteenth century saw a dramatic increase in trans-Atlantic sailing and steamship travel. As more and more ships took to sea, people became alarmed at the number of ships that sank. To reassure passengers, Traught Beck of Newark, New Jersey, fashioned a unique life jacket.

Beck's life jacket was made of rubber and could be folded and conveniently stored in closets. When the ship was in danger, the passenger stepped into the legs and pulled the suit up, slipping his arms into the sleeves.

Air pockets between the suit and its lining enabled a person to float. If the seas grew rough, the hood could be closed to keep water out. A small curved pipe allowed the person to breathe and a tiny rectangular window let him watch the action outside.

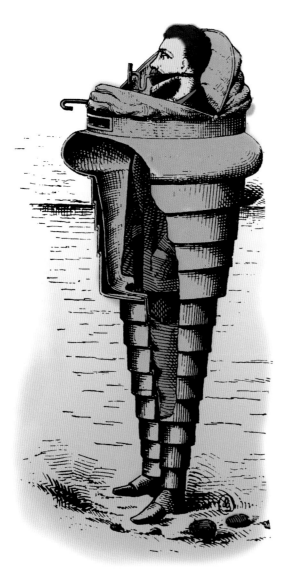

Beck realized a person might be in the water for many hours, even days. Beck put small compartments inside the suit which contained dehydrated food and fresh water to last one month. The suit was roomy enough for the wearer to slip his arms out of the sleeves and mix a cup of cold soup. He could float along, sipping his meal, and watching for a rescue ship.

This wooden stool was strapped on the wearer's back for easy carrying. When it was needed the user could sit back and relax.

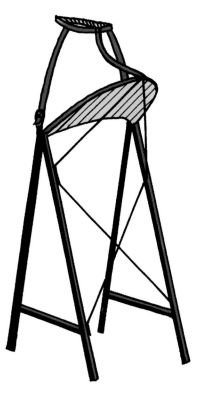

1. A portable milking stool
2. A seat for use on crowded buses, trains, and trolleys
3. A combination bustle and stool

A COMBINATION BUSTLE AND STOOL

Bustles were a common fashion item in the nineteenth century. A bustle was made of wire or whalebone and worn to extend and accent the fullness of a woman's skirt. The idea became exaggerated when some women felt that a larger bustle would be even more fashionable. Elliot Fentner of Chicago thought the extra space under the skirt could be used to conceal a handy wooden stool. If the wearer of Fentner's bustle grew tired she could lean back, and the legs of the stool would snap into position, giving her an instant seat.

The frame of this 1880 device was made of wood and worn around the neck. A rubber hose was connected to matching metal discs. Its use was as straightforward as its construction.

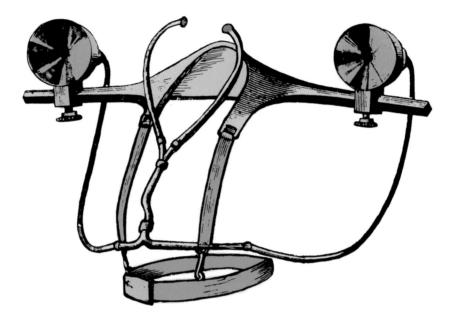

1. A hearing aid
2. A portable safety light
3. A loudspeaker
4. An insect sprayer

A HEARING AID

As the population of cities increased during the nineteenth century, so did the flow of street traffic and the resulting noise. Wagons and carriages clattered across cobblestones; horse-drawn streetcars with clanging bells rumbled along iron rails. Newfangled contraptions, called automobiles, appeared in increasing numbers. The noise seemed to come from all directions and could confuse anyone, even a seasoned traffic cop.

Professor Mayer of France felt he had a solution for this type of noise pollution. Mayer knew that all sound traveled in invisible waves; thus a traffic cop in the middle of a busy intersection really did hear sounds from all directions, front, back, and side. His invention had wide, metal discs that gathered in sound waves from only one direction. The cop would hear the traffic noise he was facing, Mayer stated in his patent, but not the noise from other directions. This would reduce the chances of his becoming distracted and keep traffic flowing smoothly.

chapter three

Getting Around

Here is a large glass ball with an iron shaft through its center. In order for this invention to work, it had to be rolling along.

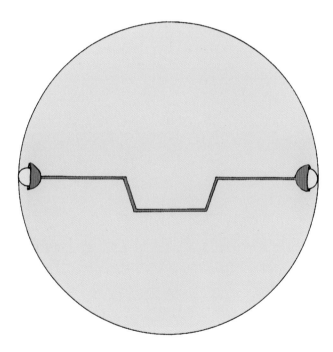

1. A device for producing lightning
2. A child's toy that automatically comes back when thrown
3. A transparent sphere for traveling
4. A giant fishbowl that rolls

A TRANSPARENT SPHERE FOR TRAVELING

The end of the nineteenth century saw an amazing boom in the popularity of bicycles. What's more, they came in a huge variety of sizes and shapes, from unicycles to two-wheelers with gigantic front tires. But they all had similar flaws. A rider had to have an excellent sense of balance, a tricky feat on bumpy dirt roads. And if it rained or snowed, the rider got wet and cold.

The inventor of this 1884 sphere was convinced that he had designed the ideal way to travel. The rider climbed inside the sphere and sat at the center of the iron shaft. Then the rider literally walked inside the sphere, causing it to roll along, building up speed gradually. To turn, all the rider had to do was lean in the direction he wanted to go. Stopping was accomplished by dragging both feet on the inside of the sphere. The rider was protected from the elements and, the inventor pointed out proudly, if he happened to come to a river, the sphere was able to float across.

It looked like a railroad car and rolled along on tracks. What's more, it was always there when you needed it.

1. A food delivery device
2. A movable ashtray
3. A portable bathtub
4. An automatic garbage pick-up and disposal unit

A FOOD DELIVERY DEVICE

Trying to stage an elegant party can be very difficult. Hiring waiters is expensive. And with people always bustling from the kitchen to the table, conversation and eating can be disrupted and chaotic. France's Gaston Menier claimed his miniature railroad system was better than a waiter.

Tracks ran from the kitchen to the table. A flat surface was attached to two cars. As each course was ready, the food was placed on the flatbed and sent out to the diners, who helped themselves. When everyone was served, the food was rolled back to the kitchen and kept warm. No fuss, no bother, no noise.

H erbert M. Small's 1889 invention was made of canvas and had four metal hooks that allowed it to be attached at both ends.

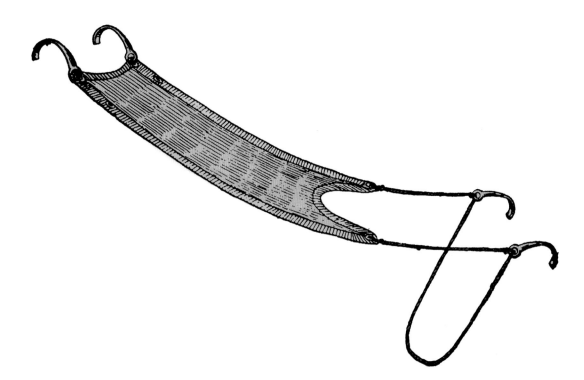

1. A bib for two sloppy eaters
2. A cloth picnic table for use in the woods
3. A device for catching leaves
4. A hammock for use on trains

A HAMMOCK FOR USE ON TRAINS

In 1840 the United States claimed a modest total of 2,818 miles of railroad track. But once the economic potential of railroads was fully understood, an absolute mania of expansion took place. The transcontinental railroad connected the East and West coasts on May 10, 1869. Scores of other rail lines pushed boldly into every developing area of the nation. By the time Small introduced his invention in 1889, there were 166,000 miles of track laid, with more to follow. Unfortunately, in the rush to expand, the comfort of the common traveler was ignored.

The rich had plush private cars and those with a few extra dollars could rent a cramped bedroom or bunk. But most people had to travel hundreds, even thousands of miles in the same uncomfortable seat.

To make sleeping somewhat more bearable, Small designed a hammock for use on trains. During the day, the canvas hammock was rolled up and stored under the seat. At bedtime, the metal hooks were attached to the backs of two seats, which allowed the user to snooze and sway through the night.

This complicated series of twisted metal rods, springs, and clamps was to be bolted onto a car.

1. An antiaccident device
2. A rake for collecting leaves in the city
3. A supersensitive AM-FM radio antenna
4. An automatic lift for car repairs

AN ANTIACCIDENT DEVICE

Heinrich Karl lived in Jersey City, a town with narrow streets and an overabundance of auto traffic. Karl must have seen a number of accidents involving cars and pedestrians, so he invented his antiaccident device in 1960.

The device was attached to the front and rear of the car, and a metal rod was secured to the brake pedal. Thick blankets or pillows were strapped to hooks on either end of the device. If a pedestrian walked in front of the car, the driver would stomp on the brakes. The movement of the brake pedal not only stopped the car, it pushed the metal rod forward, which extended the blanket about two feet. The pedestrian would receive a soft tap, Karl claimed, and if he fell backward the blanket would cushion his fall. The rakelike grills on the wheels would stop very clumsy accident victims from getting run over.

California's S. R. Mathewson wanted to help people get from one place to another quickly, comfortably, and without any upsets.

1. A steam-driven bus
2. A compact carriage for easy parking
3. A horse-drawn taxi with a heater, snack bar, kaleidoscope, and foot massager
4. A robot-operated carriage

A STEAM-DRIVEN BUS

Steam-driven cars began to appear in greater and greater numbers after 1850. These early steamers were often large contraptions whose chugging and hissing frequently frightened the horses. Horse owners were so alarmed and angered by the steamers that they pressed for laws to restrict or forbid their use.

Mathewson had an ingenious solution. He built a carriage to hold a driver and four passengers. Directly under the carriage was an exact replica of a horse. A compact five-horsepower steam engine capable of moving the carriage at eight miles per hour was inside the horse's body.

Mathewson claimed real horses would be calm when approached by a familiar-looking animal, even if it did hiss a little.

op aboard this metal device, set the small engine going, and start to pedal. You'll soon be on your way!

1. A personal portable air-conditioner
2. An automatic sailing vessel and washing machine
3. A flying machine
4. An exercise and weight-loss device

A FLYING MACHINE

People have always been fascinated by the possibility of human flight. But it wasn't until the nineteenth century that the fascination turned to passion. Thousands of designs for flying machines began to appear, most prompted by large cash prizes offered by the army.

New Haven's Dr. W. O. Ayers thought his 1885 invention would earn the prize. Two cylindrical bottles contained helium, the gas used to keep balloons floating in the air. Open a valve to fill the metal tubes with helium, which would, Ayers insisted, lift the machine off the ground. A tiny gas engine, plus the operator's foot power, turned the seven propellors, allowing the machine to go forward and backward, as well as up and down. Ayers was sure his machine would be the first to fly, though it probably rose higher in his imagination than in the air.

Eugene Baker thought up this gizmo for cars in 1930. The owner of one of these was truly ready for action.

1. An automobile gun for big game hunters
2. A magnifying glass for seeing far down the road
3. A device for talking to pedestrians
4. A high-intensity fog light

A DEVICE FOR TALKING TO PEDESTRIANS

It had happened to Eugene Baker too many times. He'd be driving down a city street when a pedestrian would cross against the light and force him to slam on his brakes. And when one pedestrian crossed against the light, others often followed. Baker and other drivers were forced to wait several minutes before they could get their cars going again.

Of course, Baker could roll down his window and yell at the pedestrians. But this wasn't pleasant during bad weather. Baker's solution was a long speaking horn that could be mounted to a car hood. When a pedestrian blocked the road, the driver leaned forward and asked him to move. Baker claimed this would startle most pedestrians into moving quickly. He also pointed up an obvious safety feature. If a pedestrian became angry, the driver was safely inside his car with the windows rolled up and doors locked!

This 1870 invention was tied securely to the two limbs of the user.

1. A pizza slicer
2. An artificial leg
3. An exercise device
4. A device for measuring distance

AN EXERCISE DEVICE

This inventor's exercise device consisted of two metal leg braces with fifteen-inch wheels attached at the bottom. Each brace had a stirrup next to the wheel. The person slipped his feet into the stirrups, then strapped the braces firmly to his legs. The exercise device worked exactly like a pair of roller skates, with the user pushing off with either the left or right foot to keep moving. An observer noted: "A space being cleared he proceeded to execute, with seemingly perfect ease, the inside and outside roll, figure eight, etc., amply demonstrating that the [exercise device] has all the capabilities of the skate, both in the variety and grace of the evolutions that can be performed with it."

chapter four

Fun and Games

First this apparatus was fastened to the wearer's wrist. Each finger was then placed in the rings. Benjamin Atkins hoped using his invention would improve the wearer's technique.

1. A mechanical finger tapper for nervous people
2. A device to help baseball players throw a curve ball
3. A five-pronged musical instrument
4. A finger-supporting device

A FINGER-SUPPORTING DEVICE

The rapid growth of American industry during the nineteenth century resulted in people having more money to spend on recreation. Neither the radio nor the television had as yet been invented, so people turned to a readily available item for fun: the piano.

Benjamin Atkins of Cinncinati, Ohio, noticed this trend and patented his finger-supporting device in 1881. The idea of his invention is very simple. Once the device was on, the five metal prongs held the fingers in a nearly horizontal position. The tips of the fingers could move a little, but not without effort. Piano teachers of the time considered these the correct position and movement for fingers, something the inventor pointed out proudly. The inventor also claimed that constant use of his finger-supporting device would increase touch and encourage perfect fingering of the piano keys.

A French engineer thought up this item in 1891. People would pay twenty francs and then have a most unusual experience.

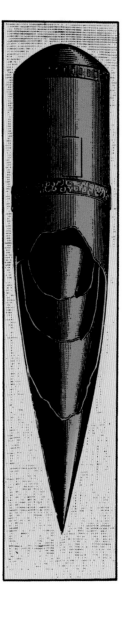

1. A floating movie theater
2. A submarine for ocean voyages
3. A machine to create sensational emotions
4. A spaceship for travel to the moon

A MACHINE TO CREATE SENSATIONAL EMOTIONS

Monsieur Carron wanted to give people a ride they would never forget. He made his metal shell 13 feet tall and 10 feet in diameter. Fifteen very brave people sat in upholstered armchairs (without seat belts!). The floor was a mattress on 20-inch springs to cushion the impact.

Once the passengers were inside and seated, the 10-ton shell was to be lifted 975 feet up the Eiffel Tower—and dropped!

"It is easy to fall 325 yards," a scientific journal of the time stated when it heard of Carron's idea, "but it has hitherto been doubtful whether one could do this and survive."

But Carron had an answer. A 180-foot-deep pond would be dug under the tower and the shell would enter the pond much as a high diver enters the water. The shell would sink over 100 feet into the pond, but air inside the metal walls would force it to rise to the surface intact, with passengers unharmed.

Brooklyn's Sidney Feist built his machine to resemble a woman. He claimed it (she) would be the perfect substitute!

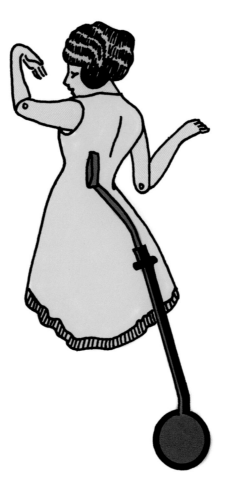

1. A dance partner
2. A robot capable of vacuuming, dusting, and other light household cleaning chores
3. An automatic mannequin for modeling dresses

A DANCE PARTNER

Feist enjoyed his weekly dance lesson, but noted that there were always more men at the class than women. Some men had to stand on the sidelines and wait for a partner to become free. He thought he'd solved the problem forever when he patented his dance partner machine in 1921.

To operate the dance partner, the man slipped his right hand into a strap in its back while holding its right hand with his left. The dance partner's other hand and arm could be bent and placed on the man's shoulder. When the man took a step the dance partner glided along on a large wooden ball. Feist maintained that his machine would help men learn to lead—and put a stop to stepped-on toes in the process.

A person was strapped into the left side of this complicated, multigeared machine. With just a little effort it helped the user get into the swing of things.

1. An automatic weight reducer
2. A device for learning to box
3. A mechanical golf instructor
4. A machine for correcting backaches

A MECHANICAL GOLF INSTRUCTOR

Hitting a golf ball straight isn't easy. A slight bend of the elbow will send the ball into the rough. If the golfer moves his hips incorrectly his ball may land in a sand trap. George Troutman patented his mechanical golf instructor in 1953. He hoped it would help golfers develop a perfect swing.

Using this strange-looking machine was surprisingly simple. First, the golfer's feet were secured in foot plates. A wide buckle went around his waist, while a cap and chin strap held his head. When the golfer took hold of the club, which was attached to a long, metal boom, he was in the correct position.

The golfer then drew back the club, ready to hit the ball. A series of rods and gears guided the movement of the golfer's hands, shoulders, hips, knees, and feet. The same thing happened when the golfer swung the club forward. Troutman felt that repeated use of his invention would let golfers feel what a proper swing was like so they could repeat it without the aid of the machine.

M r. Sivan of Switzerland was well ahead of his time when he introduced his invention in 1895. It went *tick, tick, tick* like any watch, but it did more than met the eye.

1. A miniature video game
2. A watch with no hands for practical jokers
3. A watch and compass for use at night
4. A talking watch

W illiam R. Lamb of East Greenwich, Rhode Island, took an ordinary mirror and attached a hook to it in 1894. It was a simple-looking invention, but what was it supposed to do?

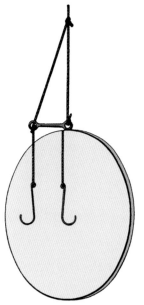

1. A device to scare campers
2. A fishing apparatus
3. A bug lure and trap
4. A mirror and hat rack

A TALKING WATCH

Mr. Sivan was a watchmaker from La Chaux-de-fonds, a village in Switzerland noted for its advances in timepieces. Sivan realized that some folks weren't always able to see their watches clearly. Some had problems with their eyesight, while others, such as miners, worked in dimly lit places.

Using Thomas Edison's advances in phonograph records, Sivan produced a small, hard rubber record. When the button on the watch was pressed, the tiny arm swung to the place on the record equivalent to the correct time. Even during the darkest night, the user would be able to hear the watch call out: "It is fifteen minutes past the hour of twelve."

A FISHING APPARATUS

Lamb felt that waiting for a fish to take the bait from an ordinary hook was time-consuming and boring. So he put a mirror at the end of his line. Bait was placed on the hook and the entire device lowered into the water.

Lamb believed that light reflecting from the mirror would attract fish quickly. In addition, the fish would then "see the reflection of himself in the mirror and be made bolder by the supposed companionship and more eager to take the bait from his competition. . . ."

A San Francisco inventor patented this contraption in 1923. It was supposed to entertain people, but it came with a real twist.

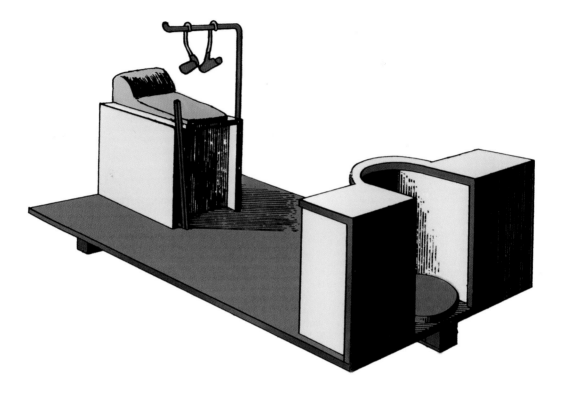

1. A walk-in video game
2. A device for listening to symphonic music while exercising
3. An arcade game with a human target
4. A one-man sailboat

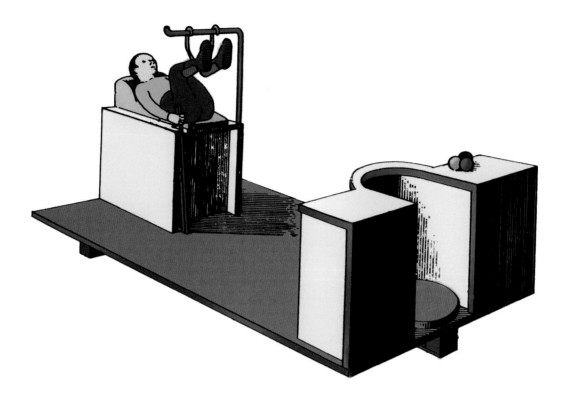

AN ARCADE GAME WITH A HUMAN TARGET

Anton Hulsman was a keen student of arcade games and human nature. He saw how much people enjoyed throwing baseballs at milk bottles and other targets. Why not let people try to hit a human!

The human target would lie on his back on a raised table with his feet secured in straps. But when the thrower was about to release the ball, the human target would grab a lever and pull. This set a series of gears under the floor in motion, which in turn made the platform the thrower was on twist around violently, making the ball go wide of its mark. Hulsman hoped his game would "induce hilarity and amusement among viewers," though he never mentioned what would happen if the person who was the target forgot to pull the lever!

This 1880 invention had four parts. One was suspended from the user's neck and strapped around his back. A second buckled on like a belt. Two pads were secured to the legs. The inventor felt his gadget would help the wearer get from one place to another in comfort.

1. A swimming device
2. A wearable cooling system for one person
3. An inflatable flying machine

A SWIMMING DEVICE

For M. Andre Gamonet of Lyons, France, swimming was too much work. Trying to cover a few hundred feet in the water was exhausting! His swimming device was the only way to travel.

This swimming device was made of rubber and inflated with air. It allowed the swimmer to float in the water in a comfortable sitting position. A handle (out of view in this illustration) turned a propellor in the rear. A swimmer could remain in the water all day, Gamonet stated, and never get out of breath.

This invention was made of wood, looked like an ordinary tree stump, and was intended for use in the forest. Harold L. Webb hoped his invention would be useful, but not in an obvious way.

1. A camouflaged heater and cooking stove for campers
2. A loudspeaker for use in state and national parks
3. A hunter's blind
4. A feeder for chipmunks, squirrels, and other small woodland creatures

A HUNTER'S BLIND

Waiting for a flock of ducks or geese to fly by can take hours. And if they spot the slightest movement, they'll quickly fly away. Tennessee's Harold Webb was so frustrated at coming home empty-handed that he invented this hunter's blind in 1961.

The enclosure was made of light plywood and could be taken apart for easy carrying. Once the hunter had chosen a spot in the woods and set up the blind, he sat inside and watched the sky through a series of slots. When the unsuspecting birds were in range, the hunter lifted the lid and aimed at his supper. For lovers of nature, Webb said his device could also be used by bird watchers and photographers.

chapter five

Personal Hygiene

Every inventor hopes to change our lives for the better. This 1924 device, made of metal or plastic with a spring mechanism in the center, was meant to do just that!

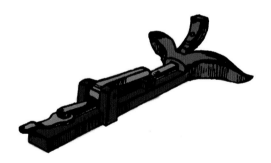

1. A combination mousetrap, whistle, and pipe
2. An automatic mustache clipper
3. An eyelash plucker
4. A device for shaping the upper lip

A DEVICE FOR SHAPING THE UPPER LIP

Fashion is constantly changing. One year short hair is in vogue; the next year it isn't. In the early 1920s it was considered quite fashionable to have full lips, then referred to as "Cupid's bow." Most women could make their lips look fuller by using bright-red lipstick. A few went so far as to have their lips surgically altered. To avoid such a drastic step, Hazel Mann of Montealegre Lola, Kansas, invented this small, easy-to-use device.

The device consisted of a handle on one end and a pair of hard rubber lips on the other. The user placed the rubber lips against her upper lip and squeezed the handle with all her might. This forced the rubber lips together like the jaws of a pliers, which pinched and reshaped the flesh of her real lip. After about five minutes, the handle could be released and, voila, a perfect "Cupid's bow" had been formed. Mann estimated the lip would hold its new shape for several hours. If the user was planning to be out in public for a longer time, she was advised to carry the device with her for instant lip reshaping.

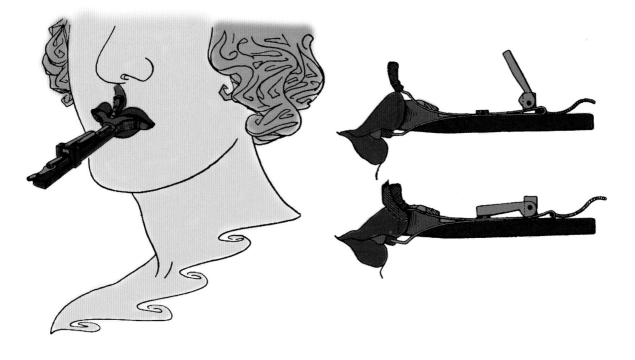

This is obviously a knife. But there's more to it than meets the eye.

1. A knife with mirror to inspect teeth
2. A knife with hollow handle to hold breath mints
3. A knife with built-in radio
4. A knife with flashlight in handle

Samuel Bligh's 1900 invention looked like a paint roller and functioned like one. But, instead of putting a substance on, this device removed something unwanted.

1. A device for cleaning between the toes
2. A beard grinder
3. A roller for massaging and removing dried skin

A KNIFE WITH MIRROR TO INSPECT TEETH

Elmer Walter of Harrisburg, Pennsylvania, wanted to do away with one of life's common embarrassments: food stuck between the teeth. Most of the time his invention, patented in 1908, functioned as an ordinary knife. But Walter had placed a mirror at the end of the knife handle. If the user wanted to inspect his teeth, a discreet tilt of the knife gave him a clear view. Many diners didn't want to interrupt their meal to walk to a bathroom to make such a check, Walter pointed out. Others would be hesitant to ask a waiter for a hand-held mirror.

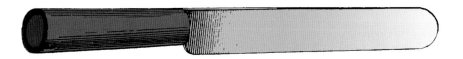

A BEARD GRINDER

Automation was a by-product of industrial growth in the nineteenth century. Bligh decided his fortune could be made with an improved method of shaving.

Bligh's roller was covered with a coating of emery, a substance that feels like coarse sandpaper. The roller was turned by a long belt that went from the center of the roller to a large, pedal-driven wheel (not shown in this picture). All the man shaving had to do was slide the roller over his face until his beard was worn away. A beard grinder meant that no soap or water was used, which, Bligh pointed out, would save a great deal of money over the years. And since no sharp blade was involved, Bligh's beard grinder was much safer than other shaving devices.

A person put one end of this tiny device in his mouth and breathed into it. A simple enough action, and one designed to prevent embarrassment.

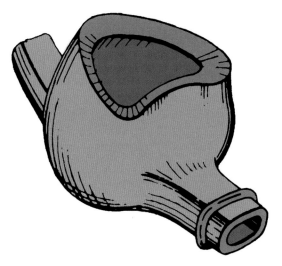

1. A smoking pipe and alarm whistle
2. A machine to stop hiccups
3. A mouth-to-mouth resuscitation device
4. An instrument to check for bad breath

Don't be fooled by this cute, cuddly, streamlined bunny. Its nose had a point that was meant to surprise you.

1. A sanitary toothpick holder for children
2. A dentist's drill
3. A hypodermic needle

AN INSTRUMENT TO CHECK FOR BAD BREATH

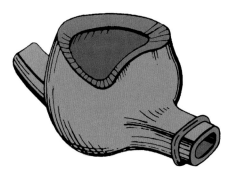

Otto M. Dyer knew that bad breath could be very embarrassing, especially at a crowded party. People often had bad breath without knowing it. Dyer's answer to the problem was patented in 1957.

His device was made of molded plastic and could be held in the palm of the hand without being seen by others. The user casually put his hand near his mouth as if to stifle a slight cough. Then he exhaled a short breath, preferably from his diaphragm. The breath was captured inside the device and a small amount escaped through a vent in the top and into the user's nose. If his breath was sweet, there was no problem. If it wasn't, the user was advised to head directly to the nearest container of breath mints.

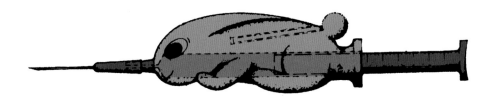

A HYPODERMIC NEEDLE

Doctor Robert Smeton, a California dentist, wanted to make visits to his office less scary for children. His solution to this age-old problem was his 1967 patent, a hypodermic needle shaped like a bunny.

The bunny's tail was removed to become a cotton swab on a stick. The tail was then dipped into a local anesthetic and applied to the patient's gums. Once sensation in the gums was deadened, a general anesthetic, such as novocaine, was injected using the "bunny" hypodermic needle. After the cavity had been filled, the sharp needle and plunger were removed from the bunny and the bunny was given to the child.

The base of this 1965 gadget was made of wood and covered with soft rubber or foam. Between the metal braces was a small platform mounted on springs. Samuel Rubin insisted his invention was the cure for some of life's everyday problems.

1. A scalp massager
2. A machine for housebreaking dogs
3. An exercise mat and trampoline
4. A surgical table with automatic anesthetic and breathing equipment

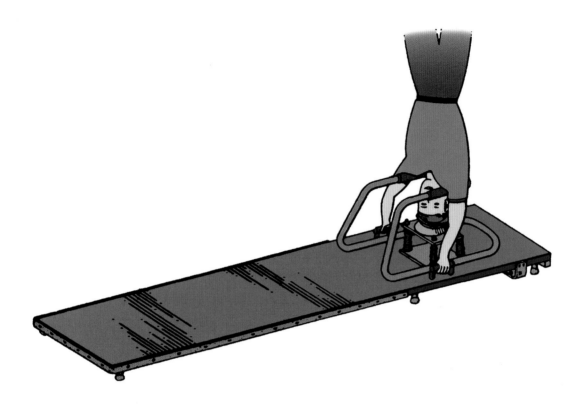

A SCALP MASSAGER

Many people believe a vigorous massage eases tense muscles. Others claim that elevating the legs to allow blood to rush to the head results in relaxation and improves mental health. Missouri's Samuel Rubin combined both ideas in his scalp massager.

A person knelt in front of the brace, placed her head in the center of the platform, grasped the handholds and rolled forward until she was standing on her head. The padded brace supported the shoulders of the user, making it easier to get into an upside-down position. The user could then give herself a head massage by turning her head left and right and by gently bouncing up and down on the platform. Do this for five or ten minutes and Rubin was certain your cares and headaches would disappear.

Alpheus Myers's 1854 invention was made of light metal with a long string tied to a loop. Myers hoped his invention would catch on.

1. A theft-proof purse
2. A tapeworm trap
3. A coffin for people being buried at sea
4. A fire escape

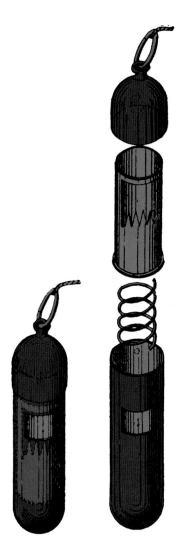

A TAPEWORM TRAP

A person can get a tapeworm by eating undercooked meat, especially pork. If the meat contains tapeworm larvae, the larva can attach itself to the wall of the intestine where the worm grows and feeds. This invention was supposed to remove tapeworms. The patient with the tapeworm was told to fast for several days. This, the inventor claimed, would make the worm very hungry. Food was placed inside the trap, then the trap was swallowed by the patient. When the worm seized the food, the movement activated a spring inside the trap, which forced tiny metal teeth into the worm's head. The doctor then pulled on the string, removing the trap and the tapeworm from the patient. If more than one tapeworm was present, the procedure was repeated. In his patent application, Myers insisted his tapeworm trap was the most reliable way to remove tapeworms. Myers didn't mention whether his cure would make the patient sicker than he already was.

This 1893 invention had soft bristles and a metal handle.

1. A battery-operated hairbrush
2. A shoe brush with built-in radio
3. A combination clothes brush, flask, and drinking cup

A COMBINATION CLOTHES BRUSH, FLASK, AND DRINKING CUP

Demands for the prohibition of alcoholic beverages echoed throughout the nineteenth century. Though usually defeated, the cry for prohibition laws became stronger after 1890. In preparation for the passage of such laws, Thomas W. Helen of Danville, Virginia, looked for ways to conceal his favorite drinks. A great deal of the time this invention posed as an ordinary clothes brush for removing lint. But the brush hid the device's true purpose. The handle was made of hollow metal and was capable of holding one pint of whiskey. When the user wanted a drink, he removed the end of the handle, which became a small cup. Undo the tiny cap and pour. Nothing could be simpler—or more secretive.

chapter six

Odds and Ends

Sebastian Lay's invention was made of metal and had padded cushions. Its most important feature, however, was that it could be folded for easy carrying.

1. A microtelevision with built-in snack tray and armrest
2. A portable sleeping cushion
3. A cane and radio

A PORTABLE SLEEPING CUSHION

Lay's 1881 invention was easy to use. The drowsy user unfolded the vertical stand and placed the sharp point in the floor. Then he rested his forehead on the upper cushion, dropped his arm on the lower one, and went to sleep. Lay felt his portable sleeping cushion would be especially welcomed by train passengers as well as by invalids who couldn't stretch out on a bed.

Chairs have been made for thousands of years. But this one, patented by Charles Singes in 1869, came with features designed to put the user at ease.

1. An air-cooled reclining rocking chair
2. A combination chair and wireless radio
3. A dentist's chair with automatic anesthesia dispenser
4. A shower chair for the infirm

AN AIR-COOLED RECLINING ROCKING CHAIR

The user of this invention sat in it as if it were an ordinary chair. What's so unusual about it? First, the person could adjust the angle he sat at by moving the toothed armrest to the desired position. Second, the seat of the chair could be rocked back and forth. Third, and most important, a bellows was located under the seat. Every time the seat tipped forward or backward it pushed down on the bellows and forced air out. The air was channeled through a metal hose and vented on the user's head. Singes insisted his chair was perfect for relaxing on hot, humid summer days.

The base of this box is made of metal, while the top is covered with thick cloth. The box has several movable parts and several uses.

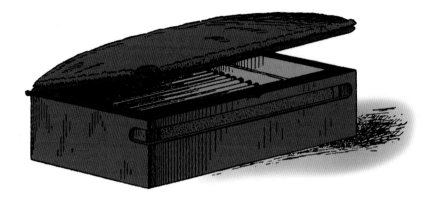

1. A coffin that plays music
2. A fire- and theft-proof jewelry box and clothes brush
3. A combination matchbox, pincushion, and mousetrap
4. A footrest and used-gum disposal unit

At mid-nineteenth century most Americans lived and worked on farms. Plows were in constant demand. This plow was patented in 1862 by C. M. French and W. H. Fancher and had a special feature that couldn't be ignored.

1. A plow with headlight for night work
2. A combination plow and cannon
3. A plow with handle for removing large rocks
4. A plow with spring-action horse prod

A COMBINATION MATCHBOX, PINCUSHION, AND MOUSETRAP

Henry Brandt made sure his 1890 invention had a variety of uses.

The padded top could be used as a pincushion. Open the lid and there was a drawer for wooden matches. The box could also be converted into a mousetrap.

The bottom of the box opened to reveal a spring and bait hook. Cheese was placed on the tiny hook. "Wee mouse walks up the bottom and nibbles the bait on the hook," Brandt explained. "The hook-lip will be tripped and instantly close the bottom of the box." The inventor was deadly serious about what to do next. To dispose of "wee mouse" the user was instructed to immerse the box in water.

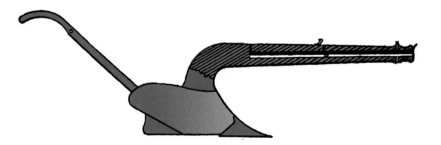

A COMBINATION PLOW AND CANNON

When this combination plow and cannon was invented, America was still largely unsettled and the Civil War raged through much of the South. This patent helped a farmer defend his property.

It functioned as a horse-drawn plow most of the time. But if the need arose, the farmer could disengage the horse, aim, and fire. "Its utility as an implement of the twofold capacity described is unquestionable," coinventors French and Fancher stated, "especially when used in border localities subject to savage feuds and guerrilla warfare."

This invention was large enough to hold one person, even if the fit was tight. It helped a lot of people rest a little more peacefully in 1868.

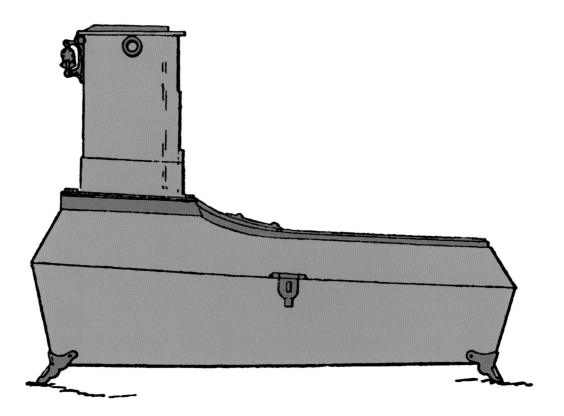

1. A one-man submarine
2. A fully enclosed bathtub and shower for the very shy
3. A heated sleeping chamber for campers
4. A coffin with escape hatch

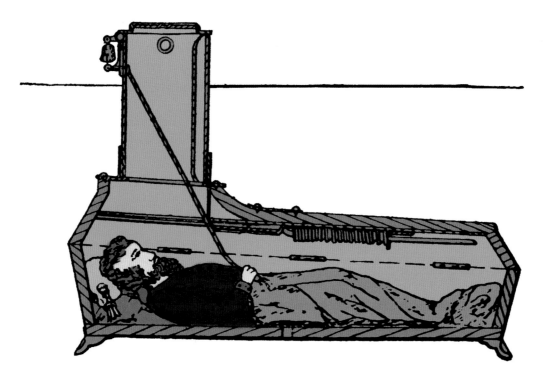

A COFFIN WITH ESCAPE HATCH

There was a time when people worried about being buried alive. The sciences of medicine and embalming were in their infancy, and once in a great while a person pronounced dead was actually in a deep coma. Newark, New Jersey's Franz Vester wanted to put those fears to rest forever.

There was nothing complicated about this invention. The deceased was buried in a coffin underground in the normal fashion. The difference was a square shaft, six to eight feet tall, that went from the top of the coffin to the ground above. A small tube at the right of the shaft provided air for breathing. If the "dead" person awoke, he had two options. He could pull a cord to ring an alarm bell. If he was able to move, he could climb a ladder inside the shaft and exit through a hatch at the top.

Attendants aboveground were instructed to peer through a glass porthole at the top of the shaft to see if the "deceased" person was alive. When they were certain he was dead, something that could take from two to four weeks, the shaft was to be removed and the hole filled in. Vester, ever a frugal man, was quick to point out that his escape hatch could be used several times.

Stanley Valinski devised this metal gadget in 1921 to solve a common problem.

1. A security device
2. A saltshaker with antispill guard
3. A mousetrap, cheese grater, and ketchup bottle

Just flip the switch of this 1971 invention and the mechanical hand takes care of the rest.

1. An automatic handball partner
2. A device for waving good-bye
3. A machine for patting a baby asleep

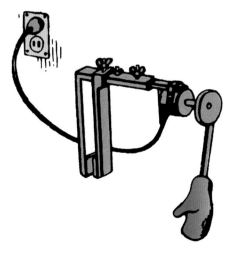

A SECURITY DEVICE

As the population in the United States rose, so did the incidence of burglary and bank robbery. But what was one security guard to do against a gang of armed robbers? Never fear! Valinski's invention was the answer.

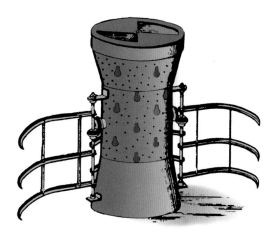

The bulletproof metal shell was six to eight feet tall and large enough to hold one person. The device was motorized so it could chase robbers and had a series of peepholes around it, allowing the security guard to see where he was going. All these features helped the guard corner the thieves. But what then? Simple. The guard pulled a lever and the mechanical arms closed around the gang, holding them until the police arrived.

A MACHINE FOR PATTING A BABY ASLEEP

One of the best ways to get a baby to sleep is to pat him on the rump. But sometimes this activity can take ten or fifteen minutes. Thomas Zelenka of California decided to take the work out of this nightly chore. He put a well-padded mitt at the end of an adjustable wooden arm. Turn on the electrical motor and the mitt swings around and around, gently and reassuringly patting the baby. In no time at all, baby will be in dreamland with no effort on the parent's part.

chapter seven

A Handful of Stories

This chapter contains five stories, a mere handful when you consider the millions of inventions that exist. We'll begin with a world-famous inventor from our colonial era and end with a little-known modern-day mechanical engineer. The problems they and the other characters in this chapter faced are as varied as the years that separate them. How each of these people solved (or didn't solve) his particular problem will give you some insight into the creative process.

One Thing Leads to Another

Benjamin Franklin was obsessively curious. When he discovered ants in his molasses pot, he devised a series of experiments to prove that ants could communicate. As his vision began to fail, he invented bifocals. Every day seemed to bring an event that stirred his imagination and creativity.

"His mind was a federation of purposes working harmoniously together," wrote Carl Van Doren, a biographer. "Other men of action might lay single plans and endlessly persist in them but Franklin met occasions as they arose and acted on them with a far-sighted opportunism."

It was this ability to take a simple fact and make something of it that set him apart, and above others of his time. Take an observation he made one day while reaching over a candle: Most of the heat from the flame rose straight up. This wasn't a particularly profound idea, since the physics of heat had been studied for hundreds of years. But in Franklin it sparked a series of logical conclusions. If most of the heat of a little candle rose straight up, then it followed that the heat from all fires did the same. And this meant the heat from a fireplace escaped up the chimney and never helped warm the room.

If ever there was anything Franklin detested it was waste, be it of time or money or heat. So Franklin, then just thirty-four years old, began thinking and tinkering, trying to find a way to maximize the heat produced by a fire. The result was an efficient cast-iron stove which he called the Pennsylvania Fireplace.

The Pennsylvania Fireplace (later to be known as the Franklin stove) had a metal air-box at the top of its heating chamber. The fire heated the air in the box, and this was vented directly into the room, not up the chimney. Franklin also learned that eliminating leaks in the heating chamber allowed him to control the amount of oxygen entering it and thus control the burning rate of the wood or coal. Franklin's fuel-efficient heating stove was introduced in 1740 and became an immediate hit.

Other inventors might have been happy to modify and sell such a stove for the rest of their lives, but Franklin wanted to concentrate full time on his newspaper. So he leased out the manufacture and sale of the stove and took only a small commission on each purchase. In fact, Franklin even refused to patent his invention.

"I declined it from a principle which has ever weighed with me on such occasions [that] as we enjoy great advantages from the inventions of others, we should be glad of an opportunity to serve others by an invention of ours, and this we should do freely . . ."

Franklin's failure to patent his invention proved to be a problem almost immediately. In an effort to cash in on the popularity of the Pennsylvania Fireplace, other manufacturers began selling inferior models that resembled the original. Franklin's response to the situation was typical: He wrote a pamphlet listing the advantages of his stove and criticizing the poorly made frauds.

The draught from one of these imitations "rushed in at every crevice so strongly as to make continual whistling and howling; and 'tis very uncomfortable as well as dangerous to sit against any such crevice."

To drive home his point to the unconvinced, Franklin added that such a stove might cause "colds, rheums, and defluxions." These, he insisted, have been known to attack the "jaws and gums, and have destroyed many a fine set of teeth in these northern colonies."

No one could compete with his stove or his words and soon the real Pennsylvania Fireplace won out over the poorly made imitations. In time this led to the development of central heating and the kitchen range.

And so, as always, Franklin had "met occasions as they arose and acted on them." The rising heat of a candle led to the invention of an efficient heating stove. And the appearance of poorly made look-alikes led to the creation of one of the first advertising campaigns in history.

Poor Johnny

It was a pleasant April afternoon in 1785, and John Fitch was walking down a country road in Pennsylvania. Around the forty-two-year-old man trees were starting to bud, wildflowers pushed their way through sodden leaves, and the chatter of birds was everywhere. But Fitch's thoughts weren't on spring or the renewal of life in the forest; Fitch was thinking about steam engines.

Not that Fitch knew much about them. He had never actually seen a steam engine, nor had he ever studied how they worked. But he'd read about them in newspapers and heard enthusiastic reports on their usefulness from friends. Steam engines were marvelous. Fire turned water to steam, the steam drove pistons up and down, and rods connected to the pistons were used to operate machinery. The labor-saving potential was astounding to Fitch.

As all these thoughts ran through Fitch's mind, a horse-drawn wagon rumbled past him. The wagon bounced along the road, growing smaller and smaller. Then something occurred to Fitch. "I was so fortunate," he would recall later, "as to have an idea that a carriage might be carried by the force of steam along roads."

Fitch spent the following days thinking over the possibilities of a steam carriage. It might work, he realized, but there would be problems. Steam engines were huge, often weighing two tons or more. How could any ordinary carriage support such weight? Then there was the problem of carrying adequate fuel and water. Finally, Fitch wasn't sure people would give up their dependable horses for a new and as yet untested machine.

"I pursued that idea about one week," Fitch went on to explain, "and gave it over as impractical." But Fitch hadn't given up on steam. Instead of a steam carriage, he began exploring the notion of a steam-powered boat.

A boat traveled on water, so it wouldn't be necessary to bring a water supply, only a hose and pump to get water to the boiler. Boats could be made large enough to hold the engine and fuel as well as passengers and cargo. Best of all, every major city in the United States was located near water, on rivers, lakes, or the ocean. A steamboat was a sure commercial bet.

Immediately, Fitch set up his Steam Boat Company and obtained monopolies from several states to operate steamboat services within their borders. Next he sought advice from notable people who were working on steam engines and obtained financing. But after this promising start, things began to sour.

He attempted to purchase a Watt engine from England in 1786, but the British government, still smarting from their defeat in the Revolutionary War, banned the sale. They even forbade the exchange of technical information on steam engines. Fitch decided to push ahead anyway.

He hired his own designers, engineers, and blacksmiths to build a steam engine of his design. Although everyone was well-intentioned and eager, the effort to build the engine took almost four years and involved a series of very costly failures.

Many people blamed the trouble on Fitch's bad luck. After all, Fitch had had an unhappy marriage, been captured by Indians, and lost his money in land speculations. Furthermore, he'd failed in past careers as a silversmith, clockmaker, and surveyor.

Others pointed to a more basic failing: his lack of technical knowledge. One of his partners in the Steam Boat Company, Henry Voight, put it bluntly: "That the Steam Boat Company miscarried was entirely owing to [Fitch's] want of Mechanism; he was the most deficient in this respect of any man I ever knew. ..."

Despite the blunderings, Fitch did manage to launch a boat powered by a steam engine in 1790. The boat was aptly called the *Perseverance*. During that summer, the boat chugged between Philadelphia and Burlington, New Jersey, carrying curiosity seekers, but almost no cargo. Shortly thereafter, the Steam Boat Company ran out of money and went bankrupt.

John Fitch had had a great idea in the steamboat (two if you count the steam carriage). He'd also had the determination to set up a company, and the energy to actually launch the first working steamboat. But his lack of a technical education cost him dearly in his trial-and-error experiments and produced an inefficient steam engine that couldn't keep his company or his ideas afloat. Fitch retired to Kentucky.

Two decades after Fitch's 1790 launching, Robert Fulton managed to purchase a Watt steam engine. He also hired British engineers to help him perfect it for use in a boat. The 1807 launching of his 150-foot-long *Clermont* earned him the nickname "father of the steamboat." Fitch's name is rarely mentioned in history books, and when it is, he's usually referred to as "Poor Johnny."

Inventing the Kitchen

Go into the kitchen and look around. Do you see anything startling? Most likely you'll find a refrigerator, stove, sink, counterspace, and shelves, plus a variety of appliances. What's so unusual about this? The organization.

Kitchens, as we know them, did not exist before the 1870s. What was referred to as a kitchen before this period was a poorly organized and hazardous work place.

The focus of an early kitchen was the open hearth where a hot fire burned constantly, even during the summer. Food was cooked on three-legged skillets or in large pots hung directly over the flames. Baking drawers were often located in the back wall of the hearth, which forced the cook, usually a woman in a long dress, to lean over the fire to check the bread. Severe scaldings and deaths from burns were commonplace.

These kitchens had no running water. To get water someone had to walk to the well or nearby stream. Because refrigerators did not exist, food had to be stored in a root cellar or suspended inside the cool shaft of the well. Bowls, pots, knives, forks, and spoons were left on the mantel above the fireplace, on tables, or in cupboards scattered around the room. There wasn't even a specific counter for cutting and mixing food.

Kitchens like this (or worse) existed for thousands of years with little change. That is, until Catherine Beecher realized the kitchen had to be redesigned.

"In most large houses," she wrote in her 1869 book, *The American Woman's Home* (coauthored with her sister, Harriet Beecher Stowe), "the table furniture, the cooking materials and utensils, the sink, and the eating room are at such distances apart that half the time and strength is employed in walking back and forth to collect and return the articles used."

Beecher's answer to these conditions was in part drawn from the ships that regularly crossed the Atlantic. Space was at a premium in these vessels, especially in the galley. The galley was a tight, cramped room and to work efficiently, in fact to work at all, everything had to be well organized and within arm's reach.

Imitate this lead, Beecher told readers. Move the water pump indoors and as close to the sinks as possible. Bins and shelving should be placed where food was to be prepared, with specific and separate storage space for pots, plates, utensils, and foodstuffs.

She also suggested homemakers do away with open-hearth cooking and use a wood-burning stove (cautioning that it be put in a room adjacent to the kitchen to lessen the heat).

It was a logical idea, but a revolutionary one. An efficient kitchen cut down the time required to cook meals and allowed women to pursue other interests. And once the concept of a centralized kitchen took hold, a whole new industry emerged, intent on making time- and energy-saving appliances and utensils.

So the next time you get yourself a glass of water, remember it was Catherine Beecher who "invented" the room you call the kitchen. Otherwise you might still be getting your drink from a well out back.

Reading Fingers

Fifty years after Johann Gutenberg perfected the printing press (circa 1450), over 10,000,000 books circulated throughout Europe. This astounding explosion of the printed word opened the world of books to all levels of society. All, that is, but one. For the blind a book was still of little use.

Hundreds of years went by before anyone even tried to help the blind read on their own. One of the first was Valentin Hauy, a French professor of calligraphy, who thought the blind might be able to read with their fingers. Hauy devised an italic typeface of the alphabet and had it embossed in raised letters on a piece of paper. By tracing the letters with his fingers, a blind reader could "see" the words.

Hauy's system was a major step forward, but it had its flaws. Running a finger along each letter took a great deal of time. The blind reader had to figure out one letter, then the next one, and so on, until he pieced together the word. In addition, the system didn't allow the blind to write.

James H. Frere's contribution was to think up the "return line." The "return line" simply meant printing lines alternately, with one running from left to right, the next with the letters reversed from right to left. This meant a reader didn't have to hunt for the beginning of the next sentence; he simply slid his finger straight down from the preceding line.

It was at this stage of the system's development that an ingenious blind boy stepped into the picture.

Louis Braille had been blinded in one eye when he inadvertently jabbed a knife into it while playing in his father's leather shop. He was three at the time, and within a few years sympathetic ophthalmia had gradually robbed him of sight in the other. Despite this, Braille became an accomplished cellist and organist, and even managed to win a scholarship to the Royal Institute for the Young Blind (founded by Haiiy in 1785).

Braille was always eager to learn, but he must have been appalled by what he found in the institute's library. It contained only fourteen books using Hauy's embossed alphabet, and these were hardly ever used by the students. Almost immediately, Braille (then only fourteen) set out to invent a truly usable system.

Braille studied the Hauy system, but could find no way to make it work to his satisfaction. He then turned to something called "night writing." Conceived by Capt. Charles Barbier, "night writing" allowed French soldiers to communicate in the dark while on the battlefield. Barbier's system used twelve raised dots grouped in different ways to represent letters and sounds. Trying to decipher the complicated twelve-dot letters was very difficult even for Braille, but he sensed the possibilities of this system.

In the months and years to follow, Braille, with help from Barbier, simplified the system to six dots with easier-to-understand groupings. This, plus the return line, allowed a blind reader to slide his fingers from line to line, deciphering the letters much more quickly. A paragraph was no longer a clump of pieced-together words; it was a smooth, flowing series of ideas and images. Braille also constructed an easy-to-use stylus and frame to allow other blind people to write with his system.

In 1825, the sixteen-year-old Braille presented his new system and writing apparatus to the amazed principal of the Royal Institute. Braille even wrote a thirty-two-page pamphlet explaining how his system could be used to represent mathematical symbols and musical notes in addition to the letters of the alphabet.

Braille's classmates liked his system and picked up its use quickly. But those in authority were hesitant about this unique way of reading. Braille was too young to really understand the problem, they insisted. And his system was too simple.

It would take until 1854 (two years after Braille's death) before the Royal Institute decided to adopt the Braille system, and an additional twenty-four years before it was given international recognition. Another fifty-four years would creep by before anyone codified the system for use by English-speaking people. Today the Library of Congress houses over 30,000 volumes in Braille, and transcribes nearly 2,000 books and 1,000 periodicals annually.

Why did it take so long to adopt the Braille system? The answer is obvious: The people who were making decisions for the blind were sighted. Because they could see they didn't really understand the problems and frustrations the blind encountered with other systems, and didn't feel their relief when using Braille's. The important thing is that Louis Braille not only "saw" the problems clearly, he also created a simple way to let his fingers read.

You Just Keep on Trying

Arthur Rayment is a mechanical engineer who's convinced he has the answer to an age-old problem: how to remove all the meat from a crab mechanically without shredding the most valuable part. Rayment's answer? A computerized robot.

For as long as people have enjoyed eating crabmeat, removing the meat from the shell has been done chiefly by hand. Typically, the pickers (almost always women) sit around a long table, heaps of the cooked crustaceans before them. Grabbing a crab in one hand, they use a paring knife or their fingers to extract the meat. The choice backfin meat comes out first and is placed in a special container. Then the remaining (and less desirable) meat is scooped out. It actually takes longer to read about the process than to do it—a good picker can clean out a shell in under twenty seconds!

There doesn't seem to be much need for machines here, and there probably wouldn't be, except that few people want to do the job anymore. The work is tedious; consider that it takes almost 100 pounds of whole crabs to produce fourteen pounds of meat. And since pickers earn between 85 cents and $1.40 per pound harvested, they have to work nonstop for many hours to make a barely decent wage. As Rayment points out, "They have to mechanize. There are fewer and fewer people prepared to sit around in nasty damp places to take out the insides of crabs."

The crab processing industry has spent many years and a lot of money to find a mechanical substitute for hand pickers. Crabs have been crushed, rolled, sucked, and vibrated to separate the meat from the shell. In all, 150 devices have been patented for crabmeat removal. Unfortunately, none of them is as good as a hand picker. J. Clayton Brooks is a Maryland processor who has himself tried to build a mechanical picker. He shakes his head sadly and says, "We learned more things that you couldn't do, that wouldn't work, than we invented that could."

Now along come Arthur Rayment and his robot. He wants the crabs to travel along a conveyer belt. An electronic eye in the robot would locate the backfin meat, then the robot would dissect the crab with special knives. "A number of methods, not just one, will be used to get out the meat," explains the inventor. Rayment is vague about the details because he hasn't been able to build and test his idea. Even so, he is positive his robot will be as good as any hand picker.

What does Brooks think about Rayment's chances for success? His comment is blunt: "I'm not holding my breath."

And what if Rayment, like the 150 other inventors before him, fails? The answer is simple: You just keep on trying till you get it right.

An Afterword

Any study of American scientific and social history will reveal the obvious—Americans have been obsessed with inventing things. Show them a bothersome problem and someone somewhere will work long hours to find the answer.

The forty-five inventions featured in this book represent some of the silliest examples of this creative energy. But isn't it nice to know that even though these inventors never became famous, their inventions still manage to affect us today—they make us smile or chuckle or laugh. And it's reassuring to know that this tradition continues. In December of 1984 William E. Bounds of Torrance, California, received patent number 4,461,234. His machine consists of a long pole attached to an electric motor. Its purpose? To relieve the arm-weary. Flip the switch and Bounds's invention will energetically and patriotically wave your American flag for you.

Where to Learn More about Inventing and Inventors

Getting a patent wasn't very hard 200 years ago. The inventor drew a picture of his machine, made a working model, and wrote a brief description of how it worked and why it was unique. Patent laws and application forms were simpler then, and determining whether an invention was new was easy.

But as the number of patents mushroomed, the process to acquire one grew increasingly more challenging, both technically and legally. Gene Amdahl and his fifteen coinventors know this from experience; their 1969 patent application set a record at 964 pages! Even searching for a particular patent can boggle the mind. There are over 4½ million patents registered, and these are divided into 300 classes and 112,000 subclasses.

The only way to cope with and learn to properly use the patent system is by being informed. The Government Printing Office has a website for kids concerning patents and patent applications. The website is www.uspto.gov/web/offices/ac /ahrpa/opa/kids.

And here's a brief bibliography of other books about inventors and inventions.

CLARK, ARTHUR C. *Profiles of the Future: An Inquiry into the Possible.* New York: Holt, Rinehart and Winston, 1984.

CLARK, RONALD W. *Edison.* New York: G. P. Putnam's Sons, 1977.

CONOT, ROBERT. *A Streak of Luck: The Life and Legend of Thomas Alva Edison.* New York: Seaview Books, 1979.

DE BONO, EDWARD. *Eureka! An Illustrated History of Inventions from the Wheel to the Computer.* New York: Holt, Rinehart and Winston, 1974.

DECAMP, L. SPRAGUE. *The Heroic Age of American Invention.* New York: Doubleday, 1961.

GILMORE, FOREST E. *How to Invent.* Houston, TX: Gulf Publishing Company, 1959.

GROSSWORTH, MARVIN. *The Mechanix Illustrated Guide to How to Patent and Market Your Own Invention.* New York: McKay, 1978.

MOORE, ARTHUR DEARTH. *Invention, Discovery, and Creativity.* Garden City, NY: Doubleday, 1969.

NORMAN, BRUCE. *The Inventing of America.* New York: Taplinger Publishing Company, 1976.

SMITHSONIAN INSTITUTION. *The Smithsonian Book of Inventions.* Washington, D.C.: Smithsonian Books, 1978.

STEIN, RALPH. *The Great Inventions.* New York: Ridge Press, 1976.

VAN DOREN, CARL. *Benjamin Franklin.* New York: Viking Press, 1938.

WILLS, GARRY. *Inventing America.* New York: Taplinger Publishing Company, 1979.